Wellness Recovery Action Plan (WRAP)
For People With Dual Diagnosis

This WRAP workbook is adapted for people who are dealing with a psychiatric illness and addictive disorder. WRAP is a system for monitoring, reducing and eliminating uncomfortable or dangerous physical symptoms and emotional feelings.

by
Mary Ellen Copeland PhD

Author of *The Depression Workbook: A Guide to Living with Depression and Manic Depression, Living Without Depression and Manic Depression: A Guide to Maintaining Mood Stability* and *Winning Against Relapse*

Contents

What is WRAP?

The *Wellness Recovery Action Plan* is a structured system for monitoring uncomfortable and distressing signs and symptoms, and, through planned responses, reducing, modifying or eliminating those signs and symptoms. It also includes plans for responses from others when your symptoms have made it impossible for you to continue to make decisions, take care of yourself and keep yourself safe.

This plan is based on empowerment and personal responsibility. It encourages you to focus on your strengths and wellness rather than on weakness and disability.

A Wellness Recovery Action Plan must be developed by the person who will use the plan. If it is developed by someone else, it is not a Wellness Recovery Action Plan.

This system was developed by people who have been dealing with a variety of psychiatric symptoms, including addictive disorders, for many years, and who are working hard to feel better and get on with their lives.

Developing a Wellness Recovery Action Plan is not a process that can be completed and forgotten. It is a day by day guide to living and will need to be changed over time as you change. Developing this plan with the support of another person or with a group can enhance the experience and increase self awareness and understanding.

2

What You Need
To Get Started

There are two things you need before you begin actually developing your plan:

1. A copy of this book that you can write in and keep, or a three-ring binder, a set of five tabbed dividers and copies of the forms. Each of the tabbed dividers will name one of the sections of the plan.
2. A list of tools—things you do or can do to help yourself feel better. This will be discussed in detail later.

Overview of a Wellness Recovery Action Plan

Befoe you begin developing your Plan, it is helpful to read through the following overview to enhance your understanding of the process.

Section 1 is a **Daily Maintenance Plan**. *Part A* is a de-
scription of how you feel when you feel well. *Part B* is a list
of everything you need to do every day to maintain your
wellness and your sobriety. *Part C* is a list of things you
might need to consider doing that day.

Section 2 deals with **Triggers**, those events or situations
which, if they occur, might cause uncomfortable symptoms
to begin or make you feel like you want to give in to your
addiction. *Part A* helps you to identify your triggers. *Part B*
is a plan of "what to do" when these triggers happen so that
symptoms or addictive behaviors will not occur .

Section 3 deals with **Early Warning Signs** and symptoms.
These are the subtle internal signs that let you know you
may be headed for a difficult time. In *Part A* you identify
your early warning signs. In *Part B* you develop an action
plan of things you can do when you notice these signs to try
and keep the situation from worsening.

Section 4 will help you identify those symptoms that occur
When Things Are Breaking Down and the situation has
gotten much worse—but has not yet reached a crisis or a
relapse, where you can still think for yourself and take action in your own behalf. *Part A* helps you recognize those
symptoms and behaviors. *Part B* is a plan of "what to do" if
any of these signs or symptoms occur.

Section 5 is a multifaceted **Crisis Plan**. It identifies those symptoms and behaviors that indicate that you can no longer make decisions, take care of yourself and keep yourself safe, and provides key information that others will need in order to make decisions for you, take action on your behalf and do things for you that will help you to recover. It is for use by your supporters and health care professionals, on your behalf. This document is also known as an *Advanced Directive*. Preparing Advanced Directives takes time and careful consideration. They cannot be developed quickly.

Part A of the Crisis Plan is information that defines what you are like when you are well as a point of reference for others who may need to refer to this plan but do not know you. *Part B* identifies those signs and symptoms that indicate others need to take over responsibility for your care. *Part C* is a list of people who you would like to take over for you in a crisis, along with those people you do not want involved. *Part D* is a listing of all medications you are currently using, those that would be acceptable to you if necessary and those that should be avoided. *Part E* is a listing of your choice of treatments and those you would like to avoid. *Part F* describes a possible home, respite center or community care option. In *Part G* you list treatment facilities that you prefer. In *Part H* you describe what your supporters can do for you that would be helpful, and those that would not be helpful. In *Part I* you list the circumstances that would show your supporters that they no longer need to follow this plan.

Developing a Wellness Toolbox

The first step in developing your own *Wellness Recovery Action Plan* is to create a *Wellness Toolbox*. This is a listing of things you have done in the past, are doing now, or would like to try to help yourself stay well. It includes things you could do to help yourself feel better when you are *not* doing well. Once you have your list you will use these "tools" throughout the developing of your WRAP.

List on the forms in this booklet, or on paper inserted in the front of your binder, the tools, strategies and skills you need to use on a daily basis to keep yourself well, along with those you use frequently or occasionally to help yourself feel better and to relieve troubling symptoms. Include things that you have done in the past, things that you have heard of and thought you might like to try, and things that have been recommended to you by health care providers and other supporters. *You can get ideas on other tools from self-help books, such as those which are listed on the resource order form at the back of this book.*

The following list includes the tools that other people have found to be useful in staying well and relieving symptoms. You may want to include some of them on your own list.

1. Talk to a friend, sponsor or counselor
2. Go to a 12-step meeting or support group
3. Talk to a health care provider
4. Peer counseling or exchange listening exercise
5. Focusing exercise
6. Relaxation and stress reduction exercises
7. Guided imagery

8. Journaling—writing in a notebook

9. Creative, affirming, and enjoyable activities

10. Exercise

11. Diet considerations

12. Light through your eyes

13. Extra rest

14. Take time off from home or work responsibilities.

15. Take medications, vitamins, minerals, herbal supplements.

16. Do something "normal" like washing your hair, shaving or going to work.

17. Get a medication check.

18. Get a second opinion.

19. Call a warm or hot line.

20. Surround yourself with people who are positive, affirming and loving.

21. Wear something that makes you feel good.

22. Look through old pictures, scrapbooks and photo albums.

23. Make a list of your accomplishments.

24. Spend ten minutes writing down everything good you can think of about yourself.

25. Do something that makes you laugh.

26. Do something special for someone else.

27. Get some little things done.

28. Repeat positive affirmations.

29. Focus on and appreciate what is happening now.

30. Take a warm bath.

31. Listen to music, make music or sing.

Your list of tools could also include things you want to *avoid*, like:

1. Alcohol, sugar and caffeine
2. Going to bars
3. Certain places in your community
4. Getting overtired
5. Certain people

Refer to these lists as you develop your WRAP and whenever you feel you need to revise all or parts of your plan.

My Wellness Toolbox

_____

_____

_____

_____

_____

_____

_____

_____

_____

_____

_____

_____

_____

_____

_____

_____

_____

_____

_____

_____

_____

_____

_____

_____

_____

_____

_____

_____

_____

_____

_____

_____

_____

_____

_____

_____

_____

_____

Section 1:
Daily Maintenance List

You may have discovered that there are things you need to do every day to maintain your wellness and recovery. Writing them down and reminding yourself to do them is an important step toward wellness and lifelong sobriety. A daily maintenance plan helps you recognize those things which you need to do to remain healthy, and then plan your days accordingly. Also, when things have been going well for a while and you notice you are starting to feel worse, it's important to be able to remind yourself of what you did to get better. When you are starting to feel out of sorts, you can often trace it back to "not doing" something on your *Daily Maintenance List.*

Use the forms at the end of this section of the book, or write "Daily Maintenance List" on the tab of your first divider, and put it in your binder followed by several sheets of binder paper.

Part A. What I'm Like When I'm Feeling Well

When you are having a hard time, it can be difficult to remember what you feel like when you are well. At these times, it helps to have a list of what you are like when you are well to refer to. On the first form or page, describe yourself when you are feeling all right. Some descriptive words that others have used are:

cheerful	reasonable	content athletic	
a chatterbox	industrious	introverted	calm
a fast learner	outgoing	competent	active
energetic	bright	optimistic	capable
contemplative	boisterous	quiet	impulsive
talkative	responsible	peaceful	spiritual
cared for	caring	connected	positive

Part B. What I Need To Do Daily To Maintain My Wellness and Sobriety

Using the next form or page in your binder, make a list of things you know you need to do for yourself every day to keep yourself feeling all right. You can also include things you want to avoid. This is the most important part of this plan for many people. They have found that if they do the things on their Daily Maintenance List they feel well more often. Their hard times become less frequent, less intense, shorter and easier to manage. Be sure your list is achievable. Don't make it so long you could never get all of the things done. In fact, you can have only one or two things on the list if that feels right to you. Following is a sample Daily Maintenance List:

- Eat three healthy meals and three healthy snacks
- Drink at least six 8-ounce glasses of water
- Avoid caffeine, sugar, junk foods and addictive substances
- Exercise for at least 1/2 hour
- Get exposure to outdoor light for at least 1/2 hour
- Take medications
- Have 20 minutes of relaxation or meditation time
- Write in journal for at least 15 minutes
- Read daily meditations
- Spend at least 1/2 hour enjoying a fun, affirming and/or creative activity
- Get support from someone who I can be "real" with (a friend, a sponsor)
- Check in with myself – how am I doing physically, emotionally, and spiritually
- Check in with my partner for at least 10 minutes
- Go to work
- Avoid bars, night clubs and liquor stores
- Avoid _____ (name people you should avoid)

Part C. Things I Should Consider Doing To Maintain My Wellness/Recovery

There may be things that you could consider doing each day—things that don't *need* to be done, but if you don't do them, you may experience stress that leads to a worsening of symptoms. On the next form or page make a reminder list for things you might need to do. Reading through this list daily, and asking yourself whether you need to do each thing, helps keep you on track. Some ideas for this list include:

- Spend some time with my counselor, case manager, sponsor, etc.
- Set up an appointment with one of my health care professionals
- Spend time with a good friend
- Spend extra time with my partner
- Be in touch with my family
- Spend time with children or pets
- Do peer counseling
- Get more sleep
- Do some housework, chores, or buy groceries
- Have some personal time
- Plan something fun for the weekend or evening
- Write some letters
- Read 12-step literature
- Repeat over and over a 12-step slogan
- Remember someone's birthday or anniversary
- Take a hot bubble bath
- Go out for a long walk or do some other extended outdoor activity (gardening, fishing, etc.)
- Plan a vacation
- Go to a support or 12-step meeting
- Simplify my life

Part A: What I'm Like When I'm Feeling Well

_____

_____

_____

_____

_____

_____

_____

_____

_____

_____

_____

_____

_____

_____

Part B: What I Need To Do Daily To Maintain My Wellness and Sobriety

_____

_____

_____

_____

_____

_____

_____

_____

_____

_____

_____

_____

_____

_____

_____

_____

_____

_____

_____

_____

_____

_____

_____

_____

_____

_____

Part C: Things I Should Consider Doing To Maintain My Wellness/Recovery

_____

_____

_____

_____

_____

_____

_____

_____

_____

_____

_____

_____

_____

_____

_____

_____

_____

_____

_____

_____

_____

_____

_____

_____

_____

_____

_____

Section 2: Triggers

Triggers are external events or circumstances that may produce signs or symptoms that are very uncomfortable. These symptoms may make you feel like you are getting ill or that you are tempted to use an addictive behavior. These are normal reactions to stressful events in your life, but if you don't respond to them and deal with them in some positive way, they may actually cause a worsening of your symptoms or a relapse. The awareness of this susceptibility, and development of plans to deal with triggering events when they come up, will increase our ability to cope, and to avoid the development of an acute onset of more serious symptoms and behaviors.

Use the form at the end of this section, or if you are using a binder, write "Triggers" on the second tabbed divider, and put it into your binder followed by several sheets of binder paper.

Part A: Identifying Triggers

List those things that might, if they happened, cause an increase in your symptoms—things that may have done so in the past or that you think would trigger them if they occurred. Following is a list of possible triggers:

- Being offered alcohol or illicit drugs
- Old "using" places, people, and things
- A friend's relapse
- Anniversary dates of losses or trauma
- Traumatic news events
- Being very over-tired
- Work stress
- Family friction

- Relationship ending
- Spending too much time alone
- Not spending enough time alone
- Being judged or criticized
- Being teased or put down
- Financial problems
- Physical illness
- Sexual harassment
- Hateful outbursts by others
- Aggressive-sounding noises (sustained)
- Being scapegoated
- Being condemned/shunned by others
- Being around an abuser, or someone who reminds me of an abuser
- Things that remind me of abandonment or deprivation
- Uncertainty
- Excessive stress
- Someone trying to tell me how to run my life
- Self blame
- Extreme guilt
- Being let down or disappointed

Part B: Triggers Action Plan

On the next form or page in your binder, make a list of things you could do to keep your symptoms from worsening if a trigger occurs. Get ideas from your Wellness Toolbox. For instance your Triggers Action Plan might include:

- Going to a 12-step or support group meeting
- Doing peer counseling
- Talking the situation over with a health care provider
- Doing a stress reduction exercise

- Playing basketball with a group of supporters
- Taking a long bath
- Writing about your feelings in your journal
- Doing something you enjoy, such as playing the piano or going fishing

Part A: Identifying Triggers

_____

_____

_____

_____

_____

_____

_____

_____

_____

_____

_____

_____

_____

_____

_____

_____

_____

_____

_____

_____

_____

_____

_____

_____

_____

_____

_____

Part B. Triggers Action Plan

_____

_____

_____

_____

_____

_____

_____

_____

_____

_____

_____

_____

_____

_____

_____

_____

_____

_____

_____

_____

_____

_____

_____

_____

_____

Section 3:
Early Warning Signs

Early Warning Signs are internal and may be un-related to stressful situations. In spite of your best efforts at reducing symptoms, you may be-gin to experience *Early Warning Signs*, subtle signs of change that indicate you may need to take some further action. If you have a dual diagnosis, warning signs can include old behaviors that were related to your drinking and drug use. Reviewing early warning signs regularly helps you to become more aware of them, allowing you to take action before they worsen.

Part A. Identifying Early Warning Signs

In this section you will list indications that a relapse might occur. Some early warning signs that others have reported include:

- Euphoric recall of past difficulties
- Denial of issues related to illness and/or addictions
- Anxiety
- Nervousness
- Forgetfulness
- Inability to experience pleasure
- Lack of motivation
- Feeling slowed down or speeded up
- Avoiding doing things on my *Daily Maintenance List*
- Being uncaring
- Avoiding others or isolating
- Making excuses

- Feeling that recovery is too hard and forgetting the positives
- Being obsessed with something that doesn't really matter
- Beginning irrational thought patterns
- Feeling unconnected to your body
- Increased irritability
- Increased negativity
- Minimizing warning signs
- Increase in smoking
- Not keeping appointments
- Spending money on unneeded items
- Impulsivity
- Poor motor coordination with no physical reason
- Dizziness
- Feelings of discouragement, hopelessness
- Passing exits on the interstate
- Failing to buckle your seat belt
- Not answering the phone
- Turning off the phone answering machine
- Overeating or under-eating
- Craving illicit drugs or alcohol
- Weepiness
- Compulsive behaviors
- Feeling worthless, inadequate
- Secretiveness
- Controlling and/or manipulative behaviors
- Being too quiet
- Easily frustrated
- Feelings of abandonment or rejection
- Feeling compelled to take too much pain medication

Part B. Early Warning Signs Action Plan

On the next form or page, develop a plan you can use to relieve these symptoms before they worsen. Use your *Wellness Toolbox* for ideas. They can be the same as, or different from, the things you would use if you were triggered. Following is a sample plan:

- Talk to my sponsor

- Arrange a visit with my counselor

- Go to two 12-step meetings each day

- Do two twenty-minute (or longer) relaxation exercises each day, which could include prayer or meditation

- Take a long walk

- Spend one hour or more doing an activity I really enjoy

- Write in my journal for at least half an hour

- Eat three healthy meals each day

- Spend some quality time with my children and spouse

- Work on changing negative thoughts to positive

- Some form of spiritual communication, such as prayer or meditation

Use the following forms to record your early warning signs, or, if you are using a binder, write "Early Warning Signs" on your third tabbed divider and fit it into your binder along with several sheets of paper.

Part A. Identifying Early Warning Signs

_____

_____

_____

_____

_____

_____

_____

_____

_____

_____

_____

_____

_____

_____

_____

_____

_____

_____

_____

_____

_____

_____

_____

_____

_____

_____

_____

_____

Part B. Early Warning Signs Action Plan

_____

_____

_____

_____

_____

_____

_____

_____

_____

_____

_____

_____

_____

_____

_____

_____

_____

_____

_____

_____

_____

_____

_____

_____

_____

_____

_____

Section 4:
When Things are Breaking Down
and Heading Toward Crisis

I n spite of your best efforts, your symptoms may prog-
ress to the point where they are very uncomfortable,
serious and even dangerous, but you are still able to
take some action in your own behalf. This is a very important time. It is necessary to take immediate action to
prevent a crisis.

Use the forms at the end of this section, or, if you are using a
binder, write "When Things are Breaking Down" (or words
that mean that to you) on your fourth tabbed divider and fit
it into your binder along with several sheets of paper.

Part A. Symptoms That Indicate Things Are Breaking Down

Make a list on the form or next page in your binder of
symptoms that indicate to you that things are getting
much worse. Remember that symptoms vary from person to
person. What may mean "things are breaking down" to one
person may mean an actual crisis to another. Others have
noted that the following symptoms indicate to them that
things are breaking down and heading toward a crisis:

- Obsessed with thoughts of addictive behaviors
- Intense cravings/urges to use alcohol or illicit drugs
- Using a "little bit" of an addictive substance
- Making efforts to obtain addictive substances

- Feeling tempted to be in touch with people I know I should avoid
- Feeling very oversensitive, fragile and needy
- Irrational responses to events and the actions of others
- Sleeping all the time
- Avoiding eating or overeating
- Wanting to be totally alone
- Racing thoughts
- Risk-taking behaviors (e.g., driving too fast)
- Thoughts of self-harm
- Obsessed with negative thoughts
- Unable to slow down
- Taking out anger on others
- Chain smoking
- Spending excessive amounts of money (specify $ amount)
- NOT feeling
- Suicidal thoughts
- Paranoia

Part B. Action Plan for Relieving Symptoms When Things are Breaking Down and Heading Toward a Crisis

On the next form or page write a plan that you think will help reduce your symptoms when they have progressed to this point. The plan now needs to be very directive, with very clear instructions and fewer choices. Following is a sample plan:

- Call my doctor or other health care provider; ask for and follow their instructions
- Call and talk as long as I need to with my sponsor or one of my supporters
- Go to three 12-step meetings

- Arrange for someone to stay with me around the clock until my symptoms subside
- Take action so I cannot hurt myself if my symptoms get worse: give my medications, money, checkbook, credit cards and car keys to a supporter
- Make sure I am doing everything on my Daily Maintenance List
- Arrange and take at least three days off from any responsibilities
- Have at least two peer counseling sessions daily
- Do three deep breathing relaxation exercises
- Do two focusing exercises
- Write in my journal for at least an hour
- Do creative activities for at least an hour each day
- Get at least 1/2 hour of aerobic exercise

Part A. Symptoms Which Indicate Things Are Breaking Down

_____

_____

_____

_____

_____

_____

_____

_____

_____

_____

_____

_____

_____

_____

_____

_____

_____

_____

_____

_____

_____

_____

_____

_____

_____

_____

_____

_____

_____

Part B. Action Plan for Relieving Symptoms
When Things are Breaking Down and
Heading Toward a Crisis

_____

_____

_____

_____

_____

_____

_____

_____

_____

_____

_____

_____

_____

_____

_____

_____

_____

_____

_____

_____

_____

_____

_____

_____

_____

_____

_____

Section 5:
Crisis Planning Or
Advanced Directives

In spite of your best planning and assertive action on your own behalf, you may find yourself in a crisis situation, a situation where others will need to take over responsibility for your care. This is a difficult situation, one that no one likes to face. You feel like you are totally out of control. Writing a *Crisis Plan* when you are well to instruct others about how to care for you when you are not well keeps *you* in control even when it seems like things are out of control. When your symptoms worsen, family members and friends may waste time trying to figure out what to do. With a Crisis Plan they will know what to do, saving everyone time and frustration, and insuring that your needs will be met. This section will guide you in developing your Crisis Plan.

A Crisis Plan needs to be developed when you are feeling well. However, you cannot do it quickly. It may take weeks or even months to come up with a good plan. Decisions like this take time and often collaboration with health care professionals, family members and other supporters. Also, you may only be able to work on it for short periods of time.

While you developed previous parts of the plan for your own use, this part of the plan is for others to use. You will want to give a copy of this plan to each of your supporters. The plan needs to be written clearly so they can understand it. You may want to discuss it with them when you give it to them so you can be sure they know exactly what you mean.

Make a copy of the Crisis Plan form. If you are using a binder, make the copy on paper that is already punched or punch it after you have made the copy. On the fifth tabbed divider write "Crisis Plan" or "Advanced Directive" and insert the copies in the binder. If you are not using a binder, develop your plan on a copy of the form in the book so you can easily copy it for your supporters. Keep your own copy in a safe place where you can easily find it when you or others need to use it.

Because this section of the plan will be copied and given to your supporters, you may want to make several copies of the form so you have one you can work on and one for the final copy.

Part A. What I'm Like When I'm Feeling Well

The first step is to describe what you're like when you're feeling well. Of course your family and friends know what you are like, but an emergency room doctor may think your ceaseless chatter, something you have always done, is a sign of mania. Or perhaps you are usually quite introverted. An unsuspecting doctor may see this as depression. Poor decision making or mistreatment could occur.

You developed this list for *Section 1* of the WRAP. You can just copy that and include it here, or you can develop a list that you feel more accurately reflects your need.

Part B. Indicators that Someone Should Take Responsibility For Me

In this section you will list those symptoms and behaviors that indicate to others that they need to take over responsibility for your care and make decisions on your behalf. You may find that this is the most difficult part of developing your Crisis Plan. This is hard for everyone. No one likes to think that they will ever have another difficult time or that others will need to take over responsibility for them or their care. And yet, through careful, well developed descriptions, if these circumstances ever come up, you stay in control even when things seem to be out of control.

Allow plenty of time to complete this section. When you start to feel discouraged or daunted, set it aside for a while.

Ask your friends, family members and health care providers for input. However, always remember that the final determination is up to you.

Be very clear in describing the symptoms. Don't try to summarize. Use as many words as it takes to describe the behavior or feeling. Following are some symptoms of crisis that others have experienced:

- Use of alcohol or drugs
- Dissociation (blacking out, spacing out, losing time)
- Bizarre behaviors (describe things you have done in the past)
- Seeing things that aren't there
- Unable to recognize family members or friends
- Incorrectly identifying family members or friends
- Unconscious or semi-conscious
- Uncontrollable pacing, unable to stay still
- Very rapid breathing or gasping for breath
- Severe agitation, where I am unable to stop repeating negative statements like "I want to die."
- Inability to stop compulsive behaviors, like constantly washing my face
- Catatonia, or not moving for long periods of time
- Neglecting personal hygiene for one or more days
- Extreme mood swings daily
- Destroying property
- Not understanding what people are saying
- Thinking I am someone I am not
- Thinking I have the ability to do something I cannot do, like fly
- Self-destructive behavior
- Abusive or violent behavior
- Criminal activity
- Threatening suicide or attempting suicide

- Not getting out of bed at all
- Refusing to eat or drink

Part C. Supporters

In this section, list those people you want to take over for you when they observe, or you tell them, that the symptoms you listed in this plan are happening. These supporters can be family members, friends or health care providers. When you first develop this plan it may be mostly health care providers. But as you work on developing your support system, try and change the list so you rely more heavily on family members and friends. Health care providers are not consistently available, and they move on to other positions. Using natural supports is less expensive, less invasive and often more comfortable.

Have at least five people on your list of supporters. If you have only one or two, they might not be available when you really need them, e.g., on vacation, sick. If you don't have that many supporters now, you may need to work on developing new and closer relationships with people by going to 12 step groups and support groups, community activities, church and/or volunteering. You may also want to reconnect with friends with whom you have lost touch. People who are responsible, calm, compassionate, understanding, honest, knowledgeable, sincere and trustworthy are usually good supporters. You may be able to think of other attributes you would like them to have.

You may want to name some people for certain tasks, like taking care of the children or paying the bills, and others for tasks like staying with you and taking you to health care appointments. When you list them, you may use the following format:

Name: Address: Phone Number:

Area of expertise or specific task I would like them to take care of:

There may be health care professionals or family members that have made decisions that were not according to your

wishes in the past. They could inadvertently get involved
in your care again if you don't include the following:

"I do not want the following people involved in any way in
my care or treatment."

Name:
Why I do not want them involved (optional):

Also, list those people you want your supporters to notify if
you are in a crisis, such as your employer or family members—along with what to tell each of them.

Many people like to include a section that describes how
they want possible disputes between supporters settled.
For instance, you may want to say that a majority needs to
agree, or that a particular person or two people make the
determination in that case.

Part D: Medication

List: 1.) the medications you are currently using and why
you are taking them, including the name of the doctor and
the pharmacy; 2.) those medications you would prefer to
take if medications or additional medications became necessary and why you would choose those; 3.) those medications that would be acceptable to you if medications became
necessary and why you would choose those; and 4.) those
medications that should be avoided and give the reasons.

Part E: Treatments

There may be particular treatments that you would like in
a crisis situation and some that you would want to avoid.
For instance, people tend to have very strong feelings about
electroshock therapy—both positive and negative. Let your
supporters know whether or not you want this treatment.
The reason may be as simple as "this treatment has or has
not worked for me in the past," or you may have some stron-
ger reservations about the safety of the treatment.

You may have also found some holistic therapies that have
helped as well as some that have not, e.g., acupuncture,

massage therapy, homeopathy. Include these in your list of treatments that help reduce your symptoms along with information on when they should be used.

Part F: Home/Community Care/Respite Center

Many people are setting up plans so that they can stay home and still get the care they need if they are in a crisis by having around-the-clock care from supporters and regular visits with health care providers. Many community care and respite centers are being set up around the country as an alternative to hospitalization where you can be supported by peers until your symptoms subside. Those who have a dual diagnosis and need help in detoxing may be able to access day detox programs. You may have to do some research and investigation to find out what is available as an option for you. You may also want to talk with other people who have used these programs.

Part G: Treatment Facilities or Hospitals

Your supporters may not be able to provide you with the home, community, respite care, or day detox you need. You may need a safe facility or hospital, you may be taking medications that need to be monitored, or you might prefer to take part in a program at a treatment facility. Using your personal experience and information you have learned through your own research or through talking with others, list those treatment facilities where you would prefer to be hospitalized if that became necessary, and list those you wish to avoid.

Part H: What Others Can Do to Help

What do you want and need your supporters to do for you that would help reduce symptoms and control unwanted behaviors—what would really help? This section takes a lot of thought. You may want to ask your supporters and other health care professionals for ideas. Take your time. Think about what was helpful in the past. Review your list of Wellness Tools and include those you think would be helpful. Different things work for different people, so your list may be very different from someone else's list. You can

also note on your list who you would like to do these things.
Some ideas include:

- Keep me away from places where I can get alcohol or illegal drugs
- Protect me from people that are upsetting
- Listen to me without giving me advice, judging me or criticizing me
- Hold me
- Let me pace
- Encourage me to move, help me move
- Lead me through a relaxation or stress reduction technique
- Peer counsel with me
- Take me for a walk
- Provide me with materials so I can draw, paint or write
- Give me the space to express my feelings
- Don't talk to me (or do talk to me)
- Encourage me
- Reassure me
- Feed me good food
- Make sure I get exposure to outdoor light for at least 1/2 hour daily
- Play me comic videos
- Play me good music (specify what kind)
- Just let me rest
- Keep me from hurting myself, even if that means you have to restrain me or get help from others
- Keep me from being abusive or hurting others

You can reduce the stress you are experiencing by including a list of specific things you need others to do for you like feed the pets, take care of the children, handle the finances, and get the mail, and who you want to do it. List the task along with the person you would like to have do it. You may want to check with them when you develop the plan to make sure they are willing to do this task if needed.

Supporters may decide that some things would help that would really be harmful. List those you have discovered to be harmful through past experience or those you feel could worsen the situation and list them in your plan.
Some examples include:

- Trying to entertain me
- Chattering
- Certain kinds of music
- Getting angry with me
- Impatience
- Invalidation
- Not listening to me
- Judging me
- Encouraging me in using addictive substances

Part I: When My Supporters No Longer Need To Use This Plan

When you feel better your supporters will no longer need to follow this plan to keep you safe. Make a list of indicators that your supporters no longer need to follow this plan. Some examples include:

- When I have slept through the night three nights
- When I eat at least two good meals a day
- When I am taking care of my personal hygiene needs
- When I can carry on a good conversation
- When I keep my living space organized
- When I can be in a crowd without being anxious
- When I am no longer trying to abuse substances

Part J. Making it Official

Many people with a history of mental illness or an addictive disorder live in fear of what will happen if they find themselves in a crisis again. They fear that they will lose the ability to make health care decisions. You can help assure that your Crisis Plan will be followed by preparing the plan as an *Advanced Directive Durable Power of Attorney (POA)* for psychiatric health care. When you develop an Advance Directive Power of Attorney, you name a person to act on your behalf. It is a proactive approach to making your own decisions about your care. This is a legal document which empowers you to name a trusted friend or family member to act as your agent, to make healthcare decisions when an attending physician determines that you have lost the capacity to make informed health care decisions for yourself. Developing a POA when healthy allows you the opportunity to openly discuss signs and symptoms of your illness, as well as your treatment preferences. When properly planned and implemented, it is a natural fit with empowerment and recovery.

Crisis Plan /Advanced Directive

To be implemented if the circumstances described on page 2 of this document occur.

Name:_____Date:_____

Part A. What I'm Like When I'm Feeling Well

_____

_____

_____

_____

_____

_____

_____

_____

_____

_____

_____

_____

_____

_____

_____

_____

_____

_____

_____

_____

_____

_____

_____

_____

_____

Part B. Indicators that Someone Should Take Responsibility For Me

If I have several of the following signs and/or symptoms, my supporters, named on the next page, need to take over responsibility for my care and make decisions in my behalf based on the information in this plan:

_____

_____

_____

_____

_____

_____

_____

_____

_____

_____

_____

_____

_____

_____

_____

_____

_____

_____

_____

_____

_____

_____

_____

Part C. Supporters

If this plan needs to be activated, I want the following people to take over for me:

Name:_____Connection/role:_____

Phone number:_____
Specific tasks for this person:

_____

_____

_____

Name:_____Connection/role:_____

Phone number:_____
Specific tasks for this person:

_____

_____

_____

Name:_____Connection/role:_____

Phone number:_____
Specific tasks for this person:

_____

_____

_____

Name:_____Connection/role:_____

Phone number:_____
Specific tasks for this person:

_____

_____

_____

Name:_____Connection/role:_____

Phone number:_____

Specific tasks for this person:

_____

_____

_____

I do not *want the following people involved in any way in my care or treatment:*

*Name:*_____

I don't want them involved because (optional):

_____

_____

*Name:*_____

I don't want them involved because (optional):

_____

_____

*Name:*_____

I don't want them involved because (optional):

_____

_____

*Name:*_____

I don't want them involved because (optional):

_____

_____

*Name:*_____

I don't want them involved because (optional):

_____

_____

Settling Disputes Between Supporters

If my supporters disagree on a course of action to be followed, I would like the dispute to be settled in the following way:

_____

_____

_____

_____

_____

_____

_____

_____

Part D. Medication

Physician:_____

Psychiatrist:_____

Other Health Care Providers:

_____

_____

_____

_____

_____

_____

_____

Pharmacy:_____

Pharmacist:_____

Allergies:_____

_____

_____

Medication or health care preparation I am using:

_____

Dosage:_____

Purpose:_____

_____

Medication or health care preparation I am using:

_____

Dosage:_____

Purpose:_____

_____

Medication or health care preparation I am using:

_____

Dosage:_____

Purpose:_____

_____

Medication or health care preparation I am using:

_____

Dosage:_____

Purpose:_____

_____

Medication or health care preparation I am using:

_____

Dosage:_____

Purpose:_____

_____

Medication or health care preparation to use if necessary:

_____

Dosage:_____

Purpose:_____

_____

Medication or health care preparation to use if necessary:

_____

Dosage:_____

Purpose:_____

_____

Medication or health care preparation to use if necessary:

_____

Dosage:_____

Purpose:_____

_____

Medication or health care preparation to use if necessary:

_____

Dosage:_____

Purpose:_____

_____

Medication or health care preparation to use if necessary:

_____

Dosage:_____

Purpose:_____

_____

_____

Medications and health care preparations to avoid*/*Why?*

_____

_____

_____

_____

_____

_____

* take special note

Part E. Treatments

*Treatment:*_____

When and how to use this treatment:

_____

_____

*Treatment:*_____

When and how to use this treatment:

_____

_____

*Treatment:*_____

When and how to use this treatment:

_____

_____

*Treatment:*_____

When and how to use this treatment:

_____

_____

*Treatment:*_____

When and how to use this treatment:

_____

_____

Treatments to avoid/ *Why?*

_____

_____

_____

_____

_____

_____

_____

_____

_____

_____

_____

_____

_____

_____

_____

_____

_____

_____

_____

_____

_____

_____

Part F. Home/Community Care/Respite Center

_____

_____

_____

_____

_____

_____

_____

_____

_____

_____

_____

_____

_____

_____

_____

_____

_____

_____

_____

_____

_____

_____

_____

_____

_____

_____

_____

_____

_____

_____

Part G. Hospital or Other Treatment Facilities

*If I need hospitalization or care in a treatment facility,
I prefer the following facilities in order of preference:*

Name:_____

Contact Person:_____

PhoneNumber:_____

I prefer this facility because:

_____

_____

Name:_____

Contact Person:_____

Phone Number:_____

I prefer this facility because:

_____

_____

Name:_____

Contact Person:_____

Phone Number:_____

I prefer this facility because:

_____

_____

Name:_____

Contact Person:_____

Phone Number:_____

I prefer this facility because:

_____

_____

Avoid using the following hospital or treatment facilities:

Name:_____

Reason to avoid using:

_____

_____

Name:_____

Reason to avoid using:

_____

_____

Name:_____

Reason to avoid using:

_____

_____

Name:_____

Reason to avoid using:

_____

_____

Part H. Help from Others

*Please do the following things that would help reduce
my symptoms, make me more comfortable and keep me*

safe:_____

_____

_____

_____

_____

_____

_____

_____

_____

_____

_____

_____

_____

_____

_____

_____

_____

_____

_____

_____

_____

_____

_____

_____

_____

_____

I need (name the person):_____

to (task): _____

_____

I need (name the person):_____

to (task): _____

_____

I need (name the person):_____

to (task): _____

_____

I need (name the person):_____

to (task): _____

_____

I need (name the person):_____

to (task): _____

_____

Do not do the following
(It won't help and it may even make things worse):

_____

_____

_____

_____

_____

_____

_____

_____

_____

_____

_____

_____

_____

Part I. Inactivating the Plan

The following signs, lack of symptoms or actions indicate that my supporters no longer need to use this plan:

_____

_____

_____

_____

_____

_____

I developed this plan on (date):_____

With the help of: _____

Any plan with a more recent date supersedes this one.

Signed: _____ Date: _____

Witness: _____ Date: _____

Witness: _____ Date: _____

Attorney: _____ Date: _____

Durable Power of Attorney:

_____

Substitute for Durable Power of Attorney:

_____

Any Personal Crisis Plan developed on a date after the dates listed above takes precedence over this document.

Section 6:
Post Crisis Planning

"I remember coming home from the hospital feeling great and as soon as I got there I was bombarded with loneliness, other people's problems and all the stuff that probably helped put me in the hospital to begin with, less the drugs and alcohol." L. Belcher

You may have found that, through developing a Wellness Recovery Action Plan and then putting it to good use, you have significantly improved the quality of your life. However, you may still have serious difficulties now and then. You may even have a crisis. You are still on the journey to recovery. This journey can get very hard from time to time. Don't give up. Before the crisis you can do some planning. You can do more planning, when you are still in crisis, as you are starting to feel better. This phase of planning, called Post Crisis Planning, will make it easier for you to take back control of your life, start doing the things you want to do and return to using your Daily Maintenance Plan as a guide to daily living.

Developing Your Post Crisis Plan

The Post Crisis Plan is different from other parts of your Wellness Recovery Action Plan in that it is constantly changing as you heal. Two weeks after the crisis you will be feeling much better than you did after one week and therefore your daily activities will be different.

As with the other parts of the Wellness Recovery Action Plan, it is up to you to decide whether or not you want to develop a Post Crisis Plan. If you decide to develop a Post Crisis Plan, it is up to you to decide when you will do it. It is most helpful if you do as much of this planning as you can when you are well. However, unlike other parts of your WRAP, some of the post crisis planning needs to be done as you are beginning to feel better after you have had a difficult time.

If you are temporarily away from your living space (in a hospital, treatment center, shelter, staying with a friend, etc.) you may want to ask staff, care providers or peers to help you with your post crisis plan. You may want to ask your sponsor or another supporter to assist you in this process. Or you could develop it on your own before you leave. A Post Crisis Plan could also be called a comprehensive discharge plan. If you are in the hospital or treatment center, you may want to ask your care providers to explain any possible discharge conditions and how these conditions would affect your Post Crisis Plan if they were imposed.

You may decide to develop your plan when you are working with a group or with your counselor. You could do it with a supportive family member or friend. Others could give you suggestions or advice if you wish, but the final word should be yours. Or you could do it by yourself. It is also up to you to decide whether or not you want to show your Post Crisis Plan to others. It may be a good idea to share your plan with people who you want to assist and support you as you heal.

In developing your Post Crisis Plan, you may find it helpful to refer to your Wellness Tools and your lists of what you are like when you are well, your Daily Maintenance Plan and your list of things you might need to do. You also may want to refer back to your Crisis Plan as you make plans to resume activities and take back responsibilities.

The forms printed here for developing a Post Crisis Plan are quite extensive. As with other sections of your Wellness Recovery Action Plan, you can skip over sections that don't seem relevant to you or that you would rather address at some other time.

You may choose to use the worksheet at the end of these forms to set up a chart with possible recovery timelines. In the first column you would write the task or responsibility you would like to resume; in the second column you would list the steps you would take to resume that task or responsibility; and in the third column, a possible day or days for accomplishing that step.

You may want to revise your plan after you have used it—especially if certain things weren't as helpful as you thought they would be, or plans did not work as you expected.

Post Crisis Plan

These words describe how I would like to feel when I have recovered from this crisis (You can refer to the first section of your Wellness Recovery Action Plan—What I am Like When I am Well):

_____

_____

_____

_____

_____

_____

_____

Post Crisis Supporters List

I would like the following people to support me if possible during this post crisis time:

Name:_____

Phone number:_____

What I need them to do:

_____

_____

_____

Name:_____

Phone number:_____

What I need them to do:

_____

_____

_____

Name:_____

Phone number:_____

What I need them to do:

_____

_____

_____

Name:_____

Phone number:_____

What I need them to do:

_____

_____

_____

Name:_____

Phone number:_____

What I need them to do:

_____

_____

_____

Arriving at Home

If you have been away from your living space, the first few hours after you return can be very important.

I would like _____ or _____
to take me to my living space.

I would like _____ or _____
to stay with me.

When I get there, I would like to _____

or_____

If the following things are in place, it would ease my return (empty bottles thrown away, place cleaned up, healthy food on hand, etc.):

_____

_____

_____

_____

_____

_____

Things I must take care of as soon as I get back to my living space (paying bills, contacting your sponsor, going to a meeting, etc.):

_____

_____

_____

_____

_____

_____

Things I can ask someone else to do for me (laundry, contacting employer, buy groceries, etc.).

_____

_____

_____

_____

_____

_____

_____

Things that can wait until I feel better (going back to work, apologizing to my friend, etc.)

_____

_____

_____

_____

_____

_____

Things I need to do for myself every day while I am recovering from this difficult time (drink 8 glasses of water a day, eat three healthy meals, get up at 7 AM, etc.).

_____

_____

_____

_____

_____

_____

Things I might need to do every day while I am recovering from this difficult time (go for a walk, call a family member, call my sponsor, go to a meeting, etc.).

_____

_____

_____

_____

_____

_____

_____

Things, people and places I need to avoid while I am recovering (certain sections of town, bars, liquor stores, certain people's homes, etc.):

_____

_____

_____

_____

_____

_____

_____

Signs that I may be beginning to feel worse (anxiety, excessive worry, overeating, sleep disturbances, cravings, negative thoughts, avoiding calling my sponsor).

_____

_____

_____

_____

_____

_____

_____

Wellness Tools I will use if I am starting to feel worse (playing my guitar, getting together with a friend, sketching, deep breathing exercises, peer counseling). Put a star in front of those that you must do. The others can be choices, depending on the circumstances.

_____

_____

_____

_____

_____

_____

Issues to Consider

What do I need to do to prevent further repercussions from this crisis—and when will I do these things? (call my employer, contact my landlord, call Protection and Advocacy, join a self help support group):

_____

_____

_____

_____

_____

_____

_____

People I need to thank:

Person:_____

When I will thank them:_____

How I will thank them:_____

Person:_____

When I will thank them:_____

How I will thank them:_____

Person:_____

When I will thank them:_____

How I will thank them:_____

Person:_____

When I will thank them:_____

How I will thank them:_____

Person:_____

When I will thank them:_____

How I will thank them:_____

People I need to apologize to:

Person:_____

When I will apologize:_____ __ ___

How I will apologize:_____ __ _____

Person:_____

When I will apologize:_____ __ ___

How I will apologize:_____ __ _____

Person:_____

When I will apologize:_____ __ ___

How I will apologize:_____ __ _____

Person:_____

When I will apologize:_____ __ ___

How I will apologize:_____ __ _____

People with whom I need to make amends:

Person:_____

When I make amends:_____ __ __

How I will make amends:_____ __ _

Person:_____

When I make amends:_____ __ __

How I will make amends:_____ __ _

Person:_____

When I make amends:_____ __ __

How I will make amends:_____ __ _

Person:_____

When I make amends:_____ __ __

How I will make amends:_____ __ _

Medical, legal, or financial issues that need to be resolved:

Issue:_____
How I plan to resolve this issue:

_____

_____

Issue:_____
How I plan to resolve this issue:

_____

_____

Issue:_____
How I plan to resolve this issue:

_____

_____

Issue:_____
How I plan to resolve this issue:

_____

_____

*Things I need to do to prevent further loss (canceling credit
cards, getting official leave from work if it was abandoned,
cutting ties with destructive friends, etc.):*

_____

_____

_____

_____

_____

_____

_____

_____

Timetable for Resuming Responsibilities

Responsibility (Examples: child care, pet care, job, cooking, household chores, etc.):
Plan for resuming this responsibility:

SAMPLE:

Responsibility: work
Plans for resuming responsibility:
1. In three days go back to work for 2 hours a day for five days
2. For one week go back to work half time
3. For one week work 3/4 time
4. Resume full work schedule

*Responsibility:*_____
Who has been doing this while I was in crisis:

_____

While I am resuming this responsibility, I need (who):____

_____

to:_____
Plan for resuming responsibility:

_____

_____

_____

_____

_____

_____

*Responsibility:*_____
Who has been doing this while I was in crisis:

_____

While I am resuming this responsibility, I need (who):____

_____

to:_____

Plan for resuming responsibility:

_____

_____

_____

_____

_____

*Responsibility:*_____
Who has been doing this while I was in crisis:

_____

While I am resuming this responsibility, I need (who):____

_____

to:_____
Plan for resuming responsibility:

_____

_____

_____

_____

_____

Responsibility:_____
Who has been doing this while I was in crisis:

_____

While I am resuming this responsibility, I need (who):____

_____

to:_____
Plan for resuming responsibility:

_____

_____

_____

_____

_____

*Responsibility:*_____

Who has been doing this while I was in crisis:

_____

While I am resuming this responsibility, I need (who):____

_____

to:_____

Plan for resuming responsibility:

_____

_____

_____

_____

_____

*Responsibility:*_____

Who has been doing this while I was in crisis:

_____

While I am resuming this responsibility, I need (who):____

_____

to:_____

Plan for resuming responsibility:

_____

_____

_____

_____

_____

Other Issues I May Want To Consider

Signs that this post crisis phase is over and I can return to using my Daily Maintenance Plan as my guide to things to do for myself every day. (Fewer cravings, positive thinking, keeping up with my personal hygiene, etc.):

_____

_____

_____

_____

_____

_____

_____

Changes in my Wellness Recovery Action Plan that might help prevent a crisis or relapse in the future:

_____

_____

_____

_____

_____

_____

_____

Changes in my Crisis Plan that might ease my recovery:

_____

_____

_____

_____

_____

_____

Changes I want to make in my lifestyle or life goals:

_____

_____

_____

_____

_____

What did I learn from this crisis?

_____

_____

_____

_____

_____

_____

Are there changes I want or need to make in my life as a result of what I have learned?

_____

_____

_____

_____

_____

If so, when and how will I make these changes?

_____

_____

_____

_____

How to Use The WRAP Program

In order to use this program successfully, when you first begin using it, you have to be willing to spend up to 15 or 20 minutes daily reviewing the pages, and be willing to take action if indicated. Most people report that morning, either before or after breakfast, is the best time to review the book. As you become familiar with your symptoms and plans, you will find that the review process takes less time and that you will know how to respond to certain symptoms without even referring to the book.

Begin with the first page in *Section 1, Daily Maintenance Plan*. Review the list of how you are if you are all right. If you are all right, do the things on your list of things you need to do every day to keep yourself well. Also refer to the page of things you may need to do to see if anything "rings a bell" with you. If it does, make a note to yourself to include it in your day.

If you are not feeling all right, review the other sections to see where the symptoms you are experiencing fit in. Then follow the action plan you have designed.

For instance, if you feel very anxious because you got a big bill in the mail or had an argument with your spouse, follow the plan in the triggers section. If you noticed some early warning signs (subtle signs that your symptoms might be worsening) like forgetting things or avoiding answering the phone, follow the plan you designed for the early warning signs section. If you notice symptoms that indicate things are breaking down, like you are starting to spend excessive amounts of money or obsessing about substance abuse, follow the plan you developed for "When Things Are Breaking Down".

If you are in a crisis situation, the plan will help you dis-
cover that, so you can let your supporters know you need
them to take over. However, in certain crisis situations, you
may not be aware or willing to admit that you are in crisis.
This is why having a strong team of supporters is so important. They will observe the symptoms you have reported
and take over responsibility for your care, whether or not
you are willing to admit you are in a crisis at that time.
Distributing your crisis plan to your supporters and dis-
cussing it with them is absolutely essential to your safety
and well-being.

If you find your plan or any part of your plan is not working for you, revise it or redo it completely. If you revise your
Crisis Plan/Advance Directive, be sure to give updated copies to your supporters and advise them of the changes.

Self-Help Resources by Mary Ellen Copeland

Books

**The Depression Workbook: A Guide to Living with Depression
and Manic Depression** Second Edition .... $19.95 x _____

**Fibromyalgia and Chronic Myofascial Pain Syndrome: A Survival
Manual** with Devin Starlanyl .... $19.95 x _____

Healing the Trauma of Abuse: A Women's Workbook
with Maxine Harris, Ph.D. .... $24.95 x _____

**Living Without Depression and Manic Depression: A Guide
to Maintaining Mood Stability** .... $21.95 x _____

The Loneliness Workbook .... $16.95 x _____

Recovering from Depression: A Workbook for Teens
with Stuart Copans, MD .... $24.95 x _____

The Worry Control Workbook .... $16.95 x _____

WRAP: Wellness Recovery Action Plan .... $10.00 x _____

WRAP for People with Dual Diagnosis .... $10.00 x _____

Plan de Acción para la Recuperación del Bienestar .... $10.00 x _____

Quantity pricing for the above WRAP books: 1-9 copies - $10 each
10-99 copies - $8 each • 100+ copies - $7 each

WRAP for Veterans and People in the Military .... $6.00 x _____

A WRAP Workbook for Kids .... $12.00 x _____

Shipping for all WRAP books: $4 for one WRAP book, plus $0.50 for each add'l copy

The WRAP Story .... Available Summer 2007
First person accounts of personal and system recovery and transformation

WRAP Software CD with printable worksheets and instructions,
contains both adult & teen versions .... $19.95 x _____

**Winning Against Relapse: A Workbook of Action Plans for
Recurring Health & Emotional Problems** Expanded version of
WRAP with suggestions for group work .... $16.95 x _____

WRAP and Peer Support: Personal, Group & Program Development
with Shery Mead .... $40.00 x _____

Quantity pricing for WRAP and Peer Support:
1-4 copies - $40 • 5-9 copies - $35 • 10-49 copies - $30 • 50+ copies - $25

Facilitator Manual: Mental Health Recovery including WRAP
Curriculum includes CD-ROM of transparencies, one WRAP book,
and complete instructions for teaching WRAP......................$129.00 x _____

Quantity pricing for Facilitator Manuals: 1-11 copies - $129 each • 12+ copies - $110 each
Manual shipping: $8 for first manual, plus $6 for each additional manual

Community Links: Pathways to Reconnection and Recovery
with Shery Mead - Program Implementation Manual & CD... $70.00 x _____

DVD and Audio Resources

Creating Wellness Workshop on DVD .... $60.00 x _____
Produced by MIEP, contains all three sessions:
   Key Concepts for Mental Health, The Wellness Toolbox, and
   Wellness Recovery Action Plan

Wellness Tools audio CD .... $19.95 x _____

WRAP: Step-by-Step audio CD .... $19.95 x _____

Subtotal: $_____

Shipping/Handling:
   $4.00 for first item, +$1.00 for each additional item: $_____
   Please use special shipping rates listed above for
   multiple WRAP books and Facilitator Manuals

Total amount due: $_____

Name: _____

Organization: _____

Address: _____

City/State: _____ Zip: _____

Phone: _____ E-mail: _____

Make checks payable to: Mary Ellen Copeland

MC or Visa #: _____

Expires: _____ 3-digit security code: _____

Mail order to: Mary Ellen Copeland
P.O. Box 301, West Dummerston, VT 05357-0301

Phone (802) 425-3660 ◆ FAX (802) 425-5580
books@mentalhealthrecovery.com ◆ www.mentalhealthrecovery.com

MENTAL HEALTH RECOVERY
Curriculum
including

Wellness Recovery Action Planning

Facilitator
Training Manual

By Mary Ellen Copeland, PhD

The *Facilitator Training Manual* with CD-ROM is an invaluable resource for anyone who is committed to sharing mental health self-help recovery information.

This comprehensive curriculum package includes:
- **Section I, Curriculum**: specific instructions for teaching recovery and WRAP in different circumstances and settings.
- **Section II, Transparencies**: both thumbnail sketches and a CD-Rom of over 200 workshop presentation transparencies.
- **Section III, Activities, Handouts and Discussion Topics**: suggestions for each topic, following the sequence of the transparencies, and handouts that may be copied and distributed.
- **Section IV, Resources**: an extensive listing of mental health resources for the facilitator.

The curriculum was originally designed for participants in training seminars. It has been revised to provide guidance to a broader audience of people teaching recovery who adhere to the values and guidelines outlined in the curriculum.

<u>Facilitator Manual: Mental Health Recovery including WRAP</u>   ____ copies at $129.00

                               Subtotal $ _____

Shipping/Handling: total # curriculum x $8.00 per item   _____

                        Total amount due _____

Name _____

Address_____

City and State _____ Zip _____

Phone_____ e-mail _____

Make checks payable to Mary Ellen Copeland.

( ) Mastercard ( ) Visa Card # _____ Expires _____

Mail order to: Mary Ellen Copeland, PO Box 301, West Dummerston, VT 05357-0301

Phone 802-254-2092   FAX 802-257-7499

E-mail: books@mentalhealthrecovery.com   Web site: www.mentalhealthrecovery.com